MEL BAY'S
BASIC HARP
for
Beginners

D1560564

By Laurie Riley

2 3 4 5 6 7 8 9 0

Table of Contents

Introduction

Playing the harp may well be one of the most satisfying things you will ever do. It is relaxing, rewarding, and you can't make a bad sound. The harp sounds beautiful when played simply, and even the most basic etudes and beginning tunes bring out the loveliness of the instrument.

After you have learned the basic techniques and tunes in this book, you can challenge yourself as much as you wish, either by taking lessons, learning from more books, tapes, and/or videos, or by teaching yourself. The harp will always have more to offer you in the many styles and techniques it can accommodate.

Each section of this book is arranged to show you the most efficient way to learn quickly and easily. If you follow the lessons carefully and in order (without skipping any section or jumping ahead and back), you will find your progress is natural and swift. Each chapter and section is of equal importance and represents an essential building block in your musical foundation, assuring that you will be able to get a lifetime of enjoyment from your harp.

The experienced musician often falls into the trap of believing that what you already know about music will carry you through the parts you choose not to read or study. This book is designed, however, for all levels, and the only part you need not read if you are already a musician is the chapter called "How to Read Music." DO pay attention to the tablature, because it contains essential information on finger placement.

There are several types of harps. The basics covered here are suitable to all of them. Your harp may be a small one or it may be a grand pedal harp; it may have wire, nylon, or gut strings. You may wish to play classical, folk, Celtic, pop, jazz, rock, gospel, or ethnic music. Be assured that all these styles are well suited to the harp.

You will hear the terms "harper" and "harpist." A harper is one who plays a traditional harp, which has no pedals. A harpist plays a classical harp (or pedal harp), which is very large and has seven pedals around its base.

The most important thing you can do in learning to play the harp is to enjoy yourself. Music is a basic part of human nature; we are all musicians deep inside! The more you allow yourself to enjoy being a musician, the better musician you will be!

The Harp

Tuning Pins

Neck

Pillar

Strings

Shoulder

Soundbox

Soundboard

Base

Feet

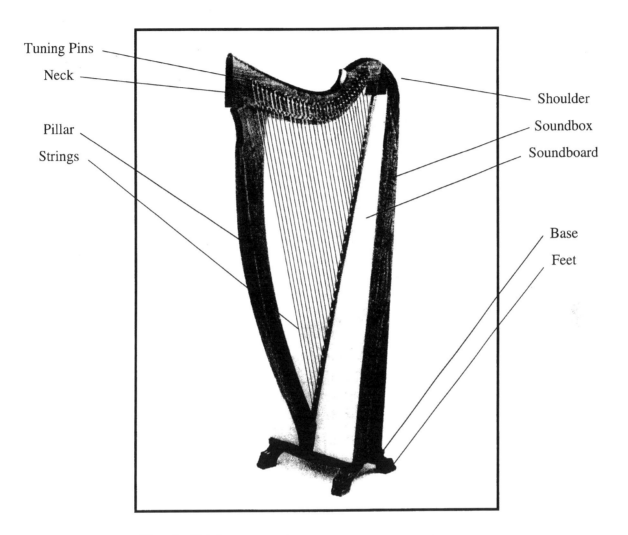

Harp by Triplett

Types of Harps

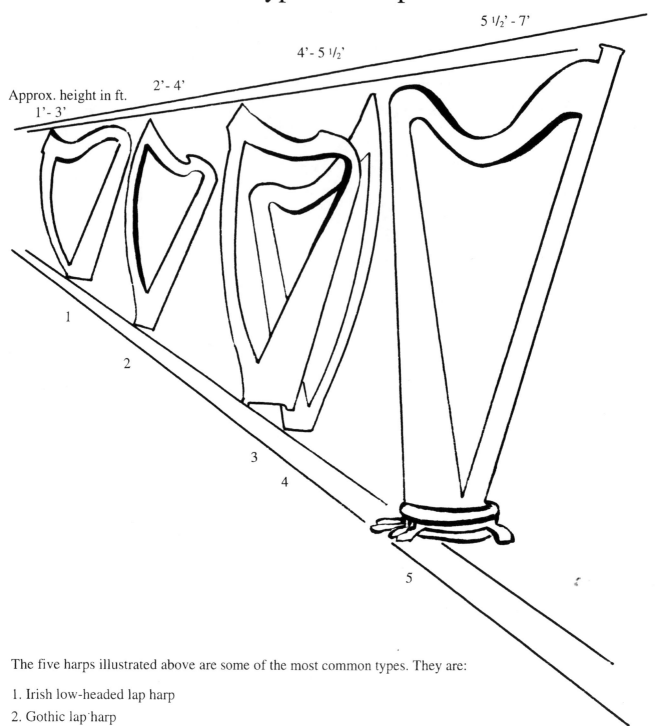

The five harps illustrated above are some of the most common types. They are:

1. Irish low-headed lap harp
2. Gothic lap harp
3. Medium-sized folk harp (these come in many shapes and sizes and can also be called Irish, Scottish, or Neo-Celtic)
4. Irish high-headed harp (usually with metal strings)
5. Pedal harp

Section 1: How To Sit With Your Harp

No matter what size your harp is, it is best to seat yourself in a comfortable way and adjust the harp to yourself rather than adjusting yourself to your harp. Since you will likely enjoy the harp so much that you will want to be able play it for long periods of time, being sure that you are comfortably seated makes good sense. You wouldn't want to limit your enjoyment of the harp by causing discomfort through awkward posture.

The best way to sit is in what is called a "neutral" position; one in which the body is comfortably balanced without any stress on any particular muscle group. Find a normal height chair, such as a kitchen chair or wooden folding chair with a level seat. Without the harp, sit toward the front edge of the seat. If your feet easily reach the floor with heels solidly down directly under the knees, the height is good.

Sit straight by rolling the top of the hips forward until you feel tall. Now you have achieved "neutral posture." It is to this position that the harp should be adjusted.

When you bring the harp to yourself, don't readjust your posture. Whatever size harp you have, it is best held with the shoulder of the harp close to your right shoulder, and the body of the harp faced slightly to the left so you can see all the strings without tilting your head.

Look at the following sections for the one that describes your harp:

THE LAP HARP: If your harp is too small to stand on the floor and is small enough to hold in your lap, it is a lap harp. This is, however, a bit of a misnomer, since holding it in your lap will usually involve enough effort to make playing less enjoyable. Find a sturdy board about 2-3 feet long and about the same width as your harp. Sit on one end of it and put the harp on the other end. If the bottom of your harp is not flat, cut out the corresponding shape on the board for the harp to fit into.

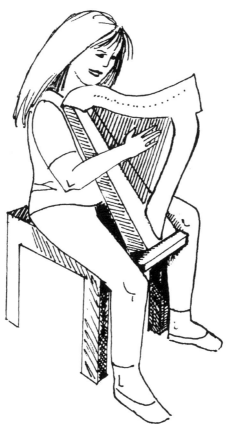

Holding the lap harp on one end of a board while sitting on the other end.

THE SMALL HARP: If your harp is a little too large to be a lap harp but not large enough to stand on the floor, it will require a stand. DO NOT SIT ON A LOW CHAIR OR STOOL, as you will eventually become very uncomfortable. Find a box, milk crate, large book, or stool that will bring the harp to the proper height.

One of my students sitting correctly with a small harp on a stand.

Harp by Hummingbird

THE MEDIUM-SIZED HARP: This is any harp whose highest point is chest-high on you when you are standing. It can stand on the floor while you sit. Simply bring it up as close as possible to yourself while properly seated. This should feel very natural and comfortable.

Medium-size harp.

Harp by Dusty Strings

If you cannot comfortably get your right arm around the body of the harp without lifting your elbow extremely, you may wish to set the harp a few inches further out in front of you and tilt it back gently onto your right knee, so the shoulder of the harp just barely touches your right shoulder.

Harp by Dusty Strings

THE LARGER FOLK HARP: This is any harp which is neck-high or higher on you when you are standing. It must be tilted back onto your knee as described above, while you sit. Read also the instructions below for the pedal harp.

THE PEDAL HARP: This is any harp with pedals; these are very large harps which must be tilted back. These harps are built to balance perfectly in the tilted position, putting no weight on your shoulder or knee. If you feel **any** weight, you have not found the balance point. Rock the harp back and forth very slowly until you feel the one place at which it feels weightless when tilted. Sit with your right knee touching it while it is balanced there. If the body of the harp does not nearly touch your right shoulder, sit on one or more pillows until you are high enough, or find a higher chair with a forward-slanted seat.

Harp by Lyon & Healy

Section 2: How to Tune Your Harp

Tuning a harp is very easy. There are several methods, most of which take only a few minutes.

When you acquire your new harp, ask to have it tuned. It will not stay tuned very long when it is new, but if it is tuned when you get it, you will be able to put it back in tune easily. After it settles in, it will need tuning every few days.

One clue that will help you in the beginning is to know that harps usually go "flat" (the pitch gets lower) when not tuned. You will usually be raising the pitch—tightening the strings—when you tune. A harp will usually only go "sharp" (higher) when left in a cold or very dry place.

NEVER allow anyone who does not know how to tune an instrument to turn the tuning pins of your harp. This will result in broken strings. It can also de-tune the harp so drastically that you may have trouble getting it back in tune if you are not experienced.

Your harp will be tuned in a diatonic (do-re-mi) scale starting from C. C is any red string. Always tune beginning with middle C, the red string closest to the middle of your harp. If you have a very small harp or are unsure which red string is middle C, ask your harpmaker.

The notes in ascending order from C are D, E, F, G, A, and B. After B there is another C, and the scale repeats. When tuning, start with middle C and work up, then go back to middle C and work down. Then double check all the strings.

The easiest method of tuning is to use an electronic tuner. These are available in music stores. There are several types. I recommend the type that has a meter and lights.

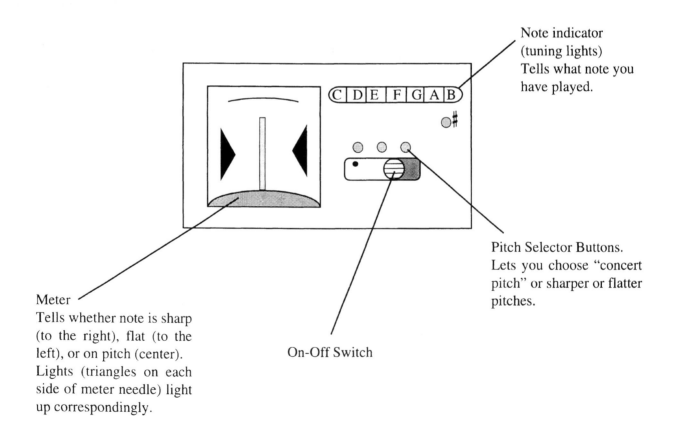

Note indicator (tuning lights) Tells what note you have played.

Pitch Selector Buttons. Lets you choose "concert pitch" or sharper or flatter pitches.

Meter
Tells whether note is sharp (to the right), flat (to the left), or on pitch (center). Lights (triangles on each side of meter needle) light up correspondingly.

On-Off Switch

USING THE ELECTRONIC TUNER: The two major features of your electronic tuner are the note indicator and the meter. The note indicator tells you which note a string is tuned to; this is a very general reading. The meter tells you whether that note is exact. First you will use the note indicator to determine what note each string is tuned to, and if it is not the correct note for that string, you will raise or lower the pitch of the string until the indicator reads the correct note. Then you will use the meter to fine-tune that note.

Pluck your middle C string. The tuner will tell you which note the string is actually producing. If your harp is out of tune, the note will be something other than C.

If the tuner reads the note as B, A, or G, the string is probably low. If it is D, E, or F, it is probably high. Using your tuning key, raise or lower the pitch of the string until the indicator reads C. (Be sure the "sharp" light is not on. C sharp is higher than C.)

Next, look at the meter. If the meter needle reads left of center, it means your C note is just a little low, and you need to tighten the string slightly to raise the pitch until the meter needle goes to the center (vice versa if the meter reads right of center).

Now pluck your D string (the one above, or shorter than, C). If the meter says it is tuned to some note other than D, repeat the above process.

Repeat this process with each string of the harp. Once you get accustomed to it, you will be pleased at how easy it is.

TUNING TO ANOTHER INSTRUMENT: The easiest instrument to tune to is a piano. It has a note for every string on your harp. Start with middle C, and playing ONLY THE WHITE KEYS, compare the sound of each note on the piano with each corresponding string on your harp. Raise or lower the pitch of your harp strings until each one sounds exactly like the notes on the piano.

If you tune to another instrument that is not a piano, tell the person playing that instrument the name of each note you need.

USING A TUNING FORK: The tuning fork gives you only one note, and you must rely on your ear to compare all the other notes with it. This method is recommended only for experienced musicians. (Even so, many experienced musicians prefer electronic tuners.)

The most common tuning forks are pitched at a "440." Hold the fork by its handle only. Tap the tynes of the fork against a hard surface and it will emit that note. While it is resonating, touch the handle of the fork firmly to the soundboard of your harp, and you will hear that note amplified. Begin tuning your harp from A. When A is in tune with the fork, use harmonics or intervals by ear to tune your middle C string.

When your middle C string is tuned, tune all the other C strings. Then compare your G's to your C's, and tune all the G's to perfect fifths from C. Then you would tune all your D strings to fifths from G. Continue tuning all the fifths until it is time to tune F. Raise all your F levers and tune them to a fifth above B. Then lower the levers. Your harp will now be in tune. (If you are very experienced, you can temper your tuning rather than using perfect fifths.)

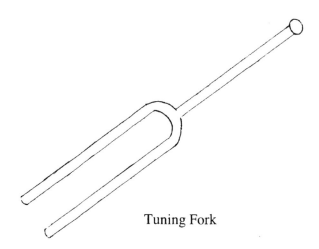

Tuning Fork

OTHER TUNING DEVICES: There are tuners available that give off an electronic sound. These noises may be on the correct pitch, but sound so dissimilar to your instrument that your result may not be accurate. The same is true of "pitch pipes," which have a crude reed which vibrates at an approximate pitch when you blow into it. I do not recommend them.

Section 3: How to Use Your Hands

The biggest favor you can do yourself as a harpist or harper is to pay attention to how you use your hands, and to develop habits of hand motion and position which will allow you to utilize all the techniques available!

Many harpers who have not paid attention to how they use their hands have ended up wondering why there are so many things they can't do! Sloppy technique turns into sloppy music. On the other hand, many students have heard horror stories about uncomfortable or difficult techniques and are afraid to learn anything about hands!

Be assured that using the hands well is comfortable, natural, and produces excellent results. At first, you will be concentrating on your hands, but soon the movements and positions become habitual, and you will be free to concentrate on the music you are making.

It is important to use the hands in a relaxed way. Structurally, certain positions allow freedom of movement and relaxation while playing, and others cause stress. The method shown here is one of the most relaxed and non-stressful positions for all sizes and shapes of hands.

Please study the illustrations carefully and compare your own hands to them as you play the harp.

NUMBERING THE FINGERS:

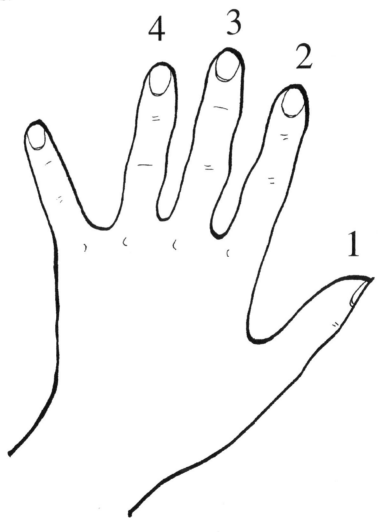

HAND POSITION

1. Always start by relaxing the hands in a "begging dog" position. This opens the spaces between the myriad tiny bones of the carpal region of the wrist and relieves pressure on the carpal tunnels and the tendons. While playing, return to this rest position briefly whenever the hand is not in use.

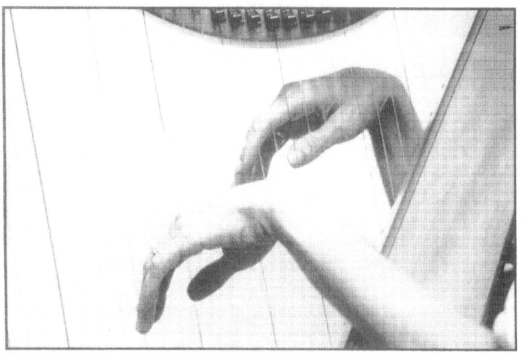

First relax the Hands.

2. Keeping the fingers completely relaxed, raise the thumbs. How far you can raise them will depend on your individual hand structure. Raise them as high as possible.

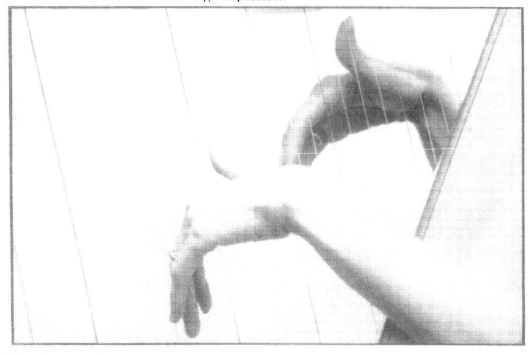

Then place the fingers while hands are still relaxed.

14

3. Approach the harp strings with the palms of your hands facing the floor. Place the thumb first as shown and relax the fingers. Notice the side of the thumb contacts the string, not the end of the thumb.

4. Place the sides of the fingertips on the strings as shown. (This part of the fingertip has the least flesh and will therefore produce the brightest tone. The end of the fingertip has more flesh and it requires more effort to pluck with all that flesh in the way.)

5. Now straighten the wrist.

6. Before plucking, squeeze all the strings. Get accustomed to doing this whenever you place your fingers, to get a solid feeling of placement and to produce a good plucking tone. You are now ready to play.

Then straighten the wrist.

PLUCKING THE STRINGS

1. Let's use the left hand first. Place the hand as shown in the illustration, following the instructions above.

2. Using the fourth finger (see finger numbers on page 13), squeeze the string.

3. While squeezing, pull the finger into the palm of your hand. This will cause the string to sound. The sound should be loud and clear. (If the string makes more noise than music, don't squeeze as hard.) Caution: do not pull the finger away from the string, or in an outward direction. This will produce a poor tone and will cause stress to the hand. Always pull inward, as though you are catching the sound in the palm of your hand and holding it there.

Be sure that ALL YOUR OTHER FINGERS REMAIN PLACED FIRMLY ON THE STRINGS while you are plucking with the fourth finger.

4. Replace the fourth finger and repeat this motion until it feels natural and comfortable and the tone is loud and clear.

5. Next, keeping the fourth finger in the palm of your hand, squeeze and pluck in the same manner with the third finger. Repeat until comfortable. Be sure to keep the second and first finger placed firmly on the strings.

6. Do the same plucking motion with the third finger, and then the second. Take your time. Relax and enjoy it.

End with a loose fist.

7. Lastly, all your fingers are in the palm of your hand and only the thumb is left on a string, where it was originally placed. The thumb squeezes in the opposite direction from the fingers. Keeping the thumb straight, move it in the direction of the squeeze and let it come to rest on the upper part of the index finger. This will cause the string to sound. You will end up with the hand in a relaxed fist; all the fingers are **in contact** with the palm of the hand.

8. Repeat all of the above steps slowly and carefully using the RIGHT HAND.

9. **Use the above steps as an exercise to develop good plucking habits.** Spend at least ten minutes repeating these plucking motions slowly and carefully each time you play. This is your time to relax and enjoy doing something beneficial that will make you a good harp player.

How the Musical Staff Compares
with the Harp and Piano

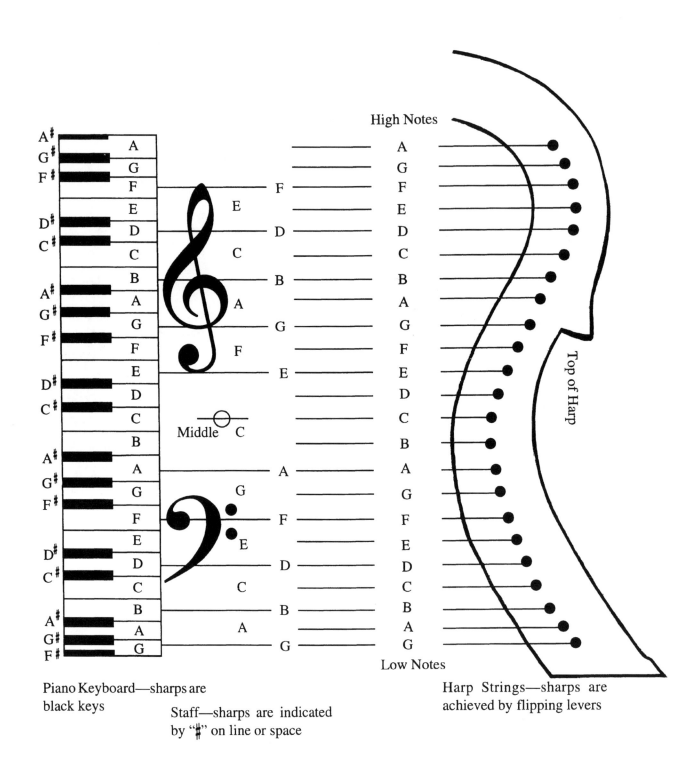

Piano Keyboard—sharps are
black keys

Staff—sharps are indicated
by "♯" on line or space

Harp Strings—sharps are
achieved by flipping levers

Section 4: How to Read Music

Musical notation is the most accurate written representation of actual music. It is composed of a staff with five lines, notes, and symbols.

The staff has five lines with four spaces; the lines and spaces are of equal importance. Most harp music will contain two staves, or "clefs," and for our purposes in this book, the lower staff (bass clef) is for the left hand, while the upper staff (treble clef) is for the right hand.

The treble clef is identified with the symbol:

Piano Keyboard—sharps are black keys

And the bass clef thusly:

Staff—sharps are indicated by "♯" on line or space

In the treble clef, the lines are lettered from the lowest line to highest: E, G, B, D, F.

The spaces of the treble clef are: F, A, C, E.

Therefore, following lines **and** spaces upward through the clef will be the notes: E, F, G, A, B, C, D, E, F.

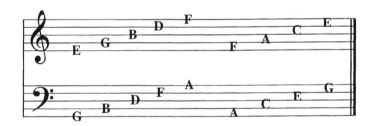

The lines of the bass clef, from the bottom up, are G, B, D, F, A.

The spaces are: A, C, E, G.

Therefore, the notes on the staff of the bass clef are: G, A, B, C, D, E, F, G, A.

The **MUSICAL NOTES** are symbols like this:

The notes appear on the lines and spaces of the staff like this:

A note which is on the first line of the treble clef staff is E. A note which is in the first space of that staff is F. And so on.

Sometimes there are notes which are too high or too low to fit on the staff. Imagine that the staff actually has more lines than are shown. The notes that are too high or too low to fit on the lines shown appear above or below the staff with a line through them or a line under or over them to show where they are relative to the staff.

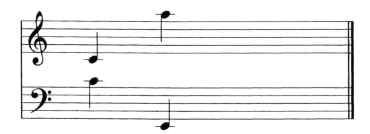

Directly in the middle between the two clefs is "Middle C." (On larger harps, the middle C string is usually also centered or nearly centered on the harp.)

A note on a staff represents the pitch and duration of a musical sound. The types of notes are:

o whole note ♩ half note ♩ quarter note ♪ eighth note

There are also sixteenth notes and thirty-second notes, which we will not be using in this beginner's book.

Sometimes eighth notes side by side will be joined like this (merely for convenience and ease of reading):

Sometimes, especially at the end of a tune, two notes will be joined like this:

This means you are to hold the note for the number of beats in both notes, rather than playing them as two separate notes.

Music consists of phrases just as speaking does. A written sentence has commas and periods as well as words. In music, the "commas" and "periods" may be written as "rests." They look like this on the staff:

A whole note or whole rest has the same duration as two half notes or half rests, four quarter notes or quarter rests, or eight eighth notes or eighth rests.

A dot after a note or rest increases its value by one half of itself.

The staff is divided into sections by "bars." The space between bars is called a "measure."

Almost all music has what we call "rhythm." That means you can tap your foot to it, dance to it, sway to it, or march to it. Musical notation clearly indicates what kind of rhythm each musical piece has, and how fast or slow it should be. At the beginning of each piece of written music you will find a "time signature" expressed as a fraction.

for example $\frac{4}{4}$ $\frac{3}{4}$ $\frac{6}{8}$ etc.

The top number indicates how many beats are in each measure. The bottom number indicates which type of note (whole, half, etc.) represents one beat.

for example $\frac{4}{4}$ = four beats per measure
                    = a quarter note is one beat

               $\frac{3}{4}$ = three beats per measure
                    = a quarter note is one beat

               $\frac{6}{8}$ = six beats per measure
                    = an eighth note is one beat

Sharps: a ♯ is called a "sharp." This symbol indicates a sharped note; if you have levers on your harp, raise the lever for the note indicated. For instance, if the sharp symbol is on the F line, sharp your F. Usually, sharp symbols will be at the beginning of the staff. Please note: the correct term for making a note sharp is "sharping," not "sharpening."

At the end of certain parts of a tune, you may see this symbol: :‖

This indicates that you are to repeat that section once.

There is a great deal more to learn about reading music. An excellent book for this purpose is Mel Bay's *Theory and Harmony for Everyone* by L. Dean Bye.

Laurie Riley and Michael MacBean

Section 5: Finger Placement

You have already seen in Section 3 how to place several fingers on the strings in preparation for actually plucking the strings. It is necessary to pre-place as many fingers as possible before each phrase of music or when playing chords. (A chord is a group of notes played together.)

The reason for doing this is for accuracy and to produce good tone. If the fingers are not pre-placed, there is little chance to squeeze each string before plucking, and the tone of lightly plucked strings will be "wimpy." Even more importantly, it is not possible to play accurately if the fingers are not in contact with the string far enough in advance of playing it; if the finger comes to the string just as the string must be plucked, you will have little confidence in your attitude or your sound. But worse, you will be using your eyes to watch your fingers find every note at the last minute instead of looking ahead to the next phrase and seeing in advance where to put your fingers next.

If you learn habitual advance placement of the fingers and learn to look ahead as you play (rather than watching the fingers play), you will become a smooth player capable of playing even the quickest and most complex passages.

On the musical notation in this book you will find brackets over groups of notes. These indicate how many notes to place in advance. The numbers corresponding with each note in the bracket are finger numbers.

They look like this:
```
 L_____
  1   2   3   4        L___
                        2  1
```

They indicate where you must pre-place the fingers.

Section 6: Use the Harp Tablature to Help You Read the Notation

Much of the music presented in this book is written in tablature as well as in regular musical notation. It is recommended that you utilize both.

Learning to read music is not difficult; and like any written language, it takes time and practice. For those who for some reason cannot learn to read music (for instance, some forms of dyslexia make it difficult or impossible), or who have not yet become proficient at music reading, the tablature may be easier to use. It should not, however, take the place of reading music for those who can. Use the tablature to clarify the music and to help yourself learn to read the music.

If you use the tablature alone, you may find it most helpful when it is used as an adjunct to an audio tape. Look at the example of tablature below:

Starting from the left, the first thing you see is the letter A in a box. This indicates "part A" of the tune. Most traditional tunes are divided into two or more parts. Learning and memorizing a tune one part at a time is much easier than trying to get through the entire tune all at once.

Next you will see the symbols "R" and "L." The "L" is always written below the "R." These indicate right-hand and left-hand. The left hand always plays one octave lower than the right when using tablature.

Following the "L" and "R" symbols you will find lines of letters indicating the names of the notes to play. In the sample above, you will see that the left hand begins first. In this case the left hand establishes a rhythm before the melody begins.

Notice the accents above some of the notes. These indicate "downbeats" or strong beats which are to be emphasized. The emphasis is in volume only, not tempo. Each note should be given the same time value (one beat), unless there is a dot after it; each dot in this type of tablature indicates the value of one beat. Therefore, a note with one dot after it should be held for two beats, and a note with two dots after it should be held for three beats. (Don't confuse the dots in this tablature with the dotted notes of musical notation. They are not the same.)

This symbol: ⌢ means two or more notes get a total of one beat (each note is worth half a beat).

The lines connecting right and left hand notes mean those notes are played at the same time. Fingering brackets are also included in the above example.

This example is one of the more advanced pieces in this book. We will start out with much easier ones, and you will become accustomed to the tablature as we progress.

Section 7: Beginning Etudes

In Section 3 we learned how to use the hands in an efficient way. After you have practiced placing the recommended hand position, you will have read about plucking the strings, and practiced doing so one finger at a time. At the end of Section 3, it is suggested that you make the plucking instructions an exercise for yourself, in order to accustom the hands to moving and plucking correctly and efficiently.

After you have thoroughly studied and practiced the section on hand position and plucking, you will be ready to go on to the following etudes.

HOW TO USE THE ETUDES:

The word "etude" is French for "study." We associate this word with a simple piece of music which, when practiced thoroughly, trains the hands for specific skills associated with your instrument.

Each etude is designed to provide new information in a step-by-step manner, so it is best to do each one in order.

Practicing your etudes is an essential part of learning to play the harp. Just being able to do each one while reading the instructions is fine, but you must also practice each one faithfully until every technique becomes habitual and can be done without conscious effort. These techniques are the building blocks of your harp-playing skill, and if they are not learned through relaxed consistent repetition, your playing will never progress beyond beginner level. Playing the harp should become easy and smooth, and should be relaxing and enjoyable. Without learning these etudes thoroughly, your playing will always involve too much effort and concentration just to get the notes right, avoid errors, count rhythms, and watch the fingers.

Each etude is designed to be played slowly and deliberately. Do not try to outsmart the exercise by speeding it up or skipping your finger placements, or the exercise will be futile. Remember that an etude is a "study."

FIRST ETUDE

Place both hands as shown in the photo.

The left hand is placed on your lowest C, E, and G notes, using fingers 3, 2, and 1 respectively. The right hand is placed the same way, one octave higher. Note we are not using the fourth fingers this time.

Squeeze all the strings slightly. Starting with the left hand, pluck the lowest note (C), closing the finger into the palm of the hand. Then pluck the second note (E). Check to be sure you did it right. Then pluck the G note with your thumb.

Proceed to the right hand and repeat what you just did with your left hand.

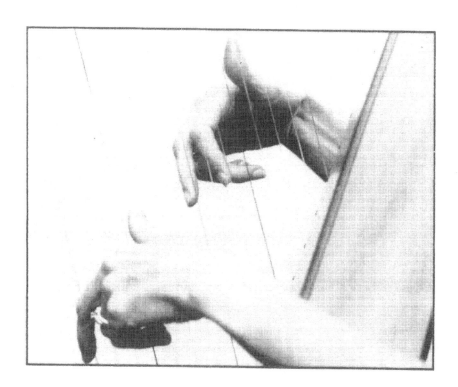

SECOND ETUDE

Place your hands as in the photo. Pluck the notes with the left hand as you did in the first etude. DO NOT PLUCK THE RIGHT HAND NOTES YET.

Before plucking with the right hand, place the left hand one octave higher than the right hand, on the same notes.

Leave the left hand where it is and carefully pluck the notes of the right hand.

Now pluck the left hand notes.

THIRD ETUDE

This etude is about how we use our eyes while playing. Rather than leaving it up to chance, we do ourselves a favor when we plan where to look, and make our eye movements just as important as our hand movements. This allows our playing to become smooth and error-free, and later will assure the ability to play faster tunes well.

This etude will make the two previous ones easier. Up to this point you probably have been carefully watching each finger do its work, placing, squeezing, plucking, and then placing a new chord. If you have practiced well, these techniques should be beginning to feel quite natural.

Now it is time to add the final touch. As you did in the second etude, place the two chords using both hands. DO NOT PLAY YET. Now that the hands are securely placed, you have no good reason to keep looking at them. You have practiced the plucking motion and no longer need to watch yourself do it. Therefore, you are free to look ahead, BEFORE YOU PLAY, to the next chord, one octave higher than the one on which your right hand is now placed. Look at the strings of that chord and keep your eyes there.

Now play the notes of the pre-placed left hand chord as usual. OOPS! Did you look at your fingers play? Probably. If so, replace that chord, look at the un-placed chord as directed above, and try again. Surprise! If your fingers are securely placed beforehand, you can easily play the notes while looking ahead!

Now place the left hand on the chord you WERE looking at. See how easy it is to find that chord now? After you have placed that chord, look up to the next un-placed chord (or if you have run out of strings because your harp is small, look down to the chord you just played).

You now have two hands placed. Play the right hand chord without looking at it. Then place it on the chord you WERE looking at. And so on. This etude will sound exactly like the second one, but it will be much easier now that you are looking ahead.

Section 8: First Tune: "The Beginner's Waltz"

The Beginner's Waltz utilizes the skills you learned in section 7. Be sure you have mastered those skills before you play this tune.

This tablature has fingering brackets; please refer to section 5 for instructions on how to use them. This is very important!

Place the hands in the position you used in section 7.

PART A: You will see that the left and right hand play part A simultaneously. First, you have two groups of three familiar notes. Practice these first. Pay close attention to the placements indicated by the brackets in the tablature. If you don't know what this means, go back and study page 24.

Next, you will see two groups of the notes D, F, and A. To place these, simply move all your fingers up one string. Be sure to place all the fingers in advance before playing these notes. Then play them just as you did the first group.

Now you will see that you must move all your fingers back down one note to the original position. Place and play these notes.

At the end of part A, the notes G E C C are played in the same position, just repeating the C.

See the information for Part B on page 30.

29

PART B: The right hand does exactly the same thing it did in part A. The left hand, however, will now pluck "chords" made up of the same notes it played before. The difference is that instead of plucking each note separately, it now plucks them all at the same time. Notice how the notes are written:

G
E   This means they are all played at the same time.
C

The lines connecting right and left hand parts indicate that the left hand chords are plucked at the same time as the downbeats (accented notes) of the right hand part.

PART C: Same as part B except now the right hand plays the chords while the left hand plays melody.

Section 9: Preparatory Etudes 4 and 5

These exercises will prepare you for playing the next tune correctly.

A: Place four fingers of the right hand. Squeeze the strings and play each note in succession as shown in the tablature. Be sure to close the fingers into the palm of the hand. Remember to keep all the fingers on the strings until the string is plucked.

B: Now move all four fingers down one note. Place and squeeze. Now pluck each note in succession as shown. Then move down again and repeat. Keep going.

C: When you have learned these skills using the right hand, then switch hands and give your left equal time.

D: Place four fingers on F G A B and pluck in succession from the lowest note to the highest.

E: Move all the fingers up one note and proceed as you did in part B, except moving up instead of down.

#4

Start with thumb (#1) on the highest note.

R: FEDC   EDCB   DCBA   CBAG

Repeat with Left hand.

BAGF   AGFE   GFED   FEDC

#5

FGAB   GABC   ABCD   BCDE

CDEF   DEFG   EFGA   FGAB

Section 10: Second Tune, "The Spider's Hornpipe"

The previous exercises will prepare you for playing this tune. Be sure to master them before attempting it.

Look first at where the accents are placed. This differs slightly from the exercise, because there are now downbeats on every other note. This changes the rhythm and feel of the music.

Emphasize the accented notes.   :‖ means repeat entire section once.   • in tablature = 1 beat that is silent.

PART A: Place four fingers as you did in the previous exercises, both right and left hand at the same time. Pluck the notes indicated, moving up one step for each group of four notes. Notice the last group has five notes. For this, place only three fingers and pluck as follows:

D	C	B	D	C	note
1	2	3	1	2	finger

PART B: Same as part A except in ascending motion. For the last group of notes use this fingering:

B	C	D	E	D
4	3	2	1	2

PART C: Now your fingers will be moving in opposite directions. The left goes up while the right moves down. Note the change at the end of the last group of left hand notes. Finger it as follows:

B	C	D	B	C
3	2	1	3	2

Note: the right hand is fingered the same way as in part A.

Section 11: "Walking Fingers"

Place fingers #1 and 2 on C and A respectively. Pluck C and place the thumb on B. Pluck A and place the finger on G. Pluck B and place the thumb on A. Pluck G and place the finger on F, etc. Always place one note before plucking the other. The motion will look like walking. (If you watch people walk, we always put one foot down before lifting the other foot up. If we had both feet off the ground between steps we'd fall down.)

Do this exercise with the right hand, the left hand, and then both hands. Do both parts (A and B).

One Hand:

Walking Fingers Two Hands:

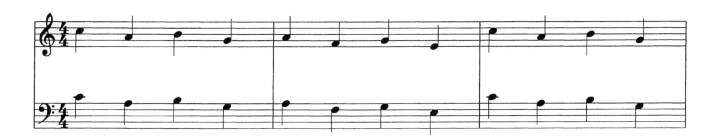

Section 12: Third Tune "Blossom Petals Falling"

In this tune the right and left hands create harmonies by playing walking sequences together in Part A, then the left hand switches to chords in Part B, and finally, in Part C, the two hands play "counterpoint," moving in opposite directions. See instructions next page.

Part A: Place fingers #1 and 2 of each hand on the first two notes. Walk down as you did in the "Walking Fingers" exercise. Note the left hand plays different notes in this piece.

Part B: Place the right hand as you did at the start of Part A. Place the left hand on the chord shown, with the third finger on A, second finger on C, and thumb (#1) on E. Pluck all three notes at the same time as you pluck the corresponding note (C) in the right hand. Follow the tablature.

Part C: Place the right hand on C, E, and G all at once. Place the left hand on G, E, and C all at once. Play the first four notes with both hands, keeping the fingers placed until the notes are plucked. Then switch to the next group of notes and do the same thing. Lastly, move back to the original group of notes and repeat.

Section 13: Non-Threatening Theory

You've probably noticed the use of words like "chord" and "octave" which have become unavoidable at this point in your progress. It's time for us to find out what these words mean and why we use them. "Theory" is the term applied to musical terminology and the reasons for that terminology.

THE SCALE

Sit at your harp. Look at a red string (C). Now count up the strings from one red string to another. You already know the names of the strings (see Section 2), C, D, E, F, G, A, B, C. If you call C "string #1," then all the C's must be 1's. Every string has both a number and a letter for identification. You would count this way:

C	D	E	F	G	A	B	C
1	2	3	4	5	6	7	1(8)

You can think of the scale as a repeating circle, like this:

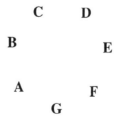

OCTAVES

The distance from C to C, or 1 to 1, is an OCTAVE.

The distance from D to D, or 2 to 2, is also an OCTAVE, and so on. The distance from any note to the next note of the same name is always an octave.

INTERVALS

Two notes sounding at the same time is called an INTERVAL. There are seven kinds of intervals. They are quite simple. For instance, look at strings 1 and 2. Pluck them separately and then together. The distance between them is from 1 to 2, therefore this interval is called a "second." We can think of intervals as "the distance between two notes."

Now look at strings 1 and 3. Pluck them. This interval is called a "third." From 1 to 4 is a "fourth." And so on. You can go all the way to a "seventh," and after that you will have an "octave."

In the "Walking Fingers" exercise, you walked down and up the strings in intervals of thirds. Thirds have a very pleasing sound to us. Each different kind of interval has a characteristic sound and can be used for different effects.

CHORDS

Now look at strings 1, 3, and 5. Place your fingers on them as you did in "Blossom Petals Falling." Now pluck the notes separately, and then try them all at once. This is a CHORD. A chord is more than two notes sounding at the same time.

Chords contain intervals. For instance, the chord you just played has a third from C to E and another third from E to G. It also has a fifth from C to G.

If C is 1, the string numbers of your chord are 1-3-5. This is the simplest form of a chord. The name of this chord is "C." It is also called the "one" chord because it starts on the first note of the scale. The numbers of chords are written in Roman Numerals to distinguish then from string numbers. (C=I, D=II, E=III, F=IV, G=V, etc.)

Please see the chart in section 18 to clarify intervals and chords.

We will explore more about theory in later sections.

Section 14: Crossovers and Scales

In this section we will look at the easiest way to play a scale going down. (A "scale" is all the consecutive notes in an octave.) A scale has seven notes:

going up: going down:

C, D, E, F, G, A, B, C   C, B, A, G, F, E, D, C
1 2 3 4 5 67 1   1 7 6 5 4 3 2 1

Yet we can only use four fingers at a time. If you start a scale on finger #4 (going up), you run out of fingers before the scale is done. Since all the fingers have been used, they are no longer on the strings, so you could just re-place them on the next group of notes. But there is a more accurate and smoother way. It is called "crossovers." Look at the exercise:

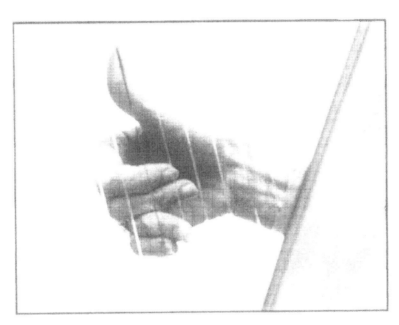

R: } C B A G ⌢F E D C ⌢B A G F ⌢E D C B ⌢A G F E ⌢D C B A etc.
L: }

finger number   1 2 3 4⌢1 2 3 4⌢1 2 34⌢1 234⌢1 234⌢1 234

The curved line connecting each group of four notes indicates a crossover.

Place four fingers on the first four notes indicated in the tablature like this:

    C   B   A   G
    1   2   3   4

After plucking the first three notes, finger #4 remains on G. Reaching up with the thumb, cross over finger #4 and place the thumb on F. Keep as much distance as you can between finger and thumb.

Pluck G with the 4th finger, and place fingers 2, 3, and 4 on the strings below the thumb. Pluck consecutively. Continue down the scale in the same way.

39

Section 15: Fourth Tune, "Cathedral Bells"

Notice the "rest" in the last measure in the bass clef. The rest simply means don't play those beats.

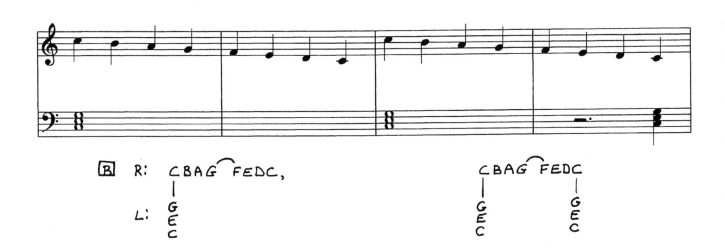

PART A: Play the notes with both right and left hands at the same time, making the indicated crossovers and using the same finger placements as in the exercise on page 39.

PART B: The right hand repeats part A while the left plays chords as indicated.

Section 16: More Easy Theory

To continue our previous discussion of chords, look at the chart below. The lines represent strings. The string names are at the top and their corresponding numbers at the bottom. On the left are Roman Numerals representing chord numbers, with the names of those chords (C, D, E, etc.) if the harp is tuned in a diatonic C scale as shown in Section 1 on tuning the harp. (When the harp is tuned to another scale, the chord names corresponding with the numbers are different).

An x represents a placed finger and/or a plucked note.

To play a C (I) chord, place the fingers as shown on C, E, and G, and then pluck those notes.

To play a D (II) chord, place the fingers as shown on D, F, and A, and pluck those notes. And so on.

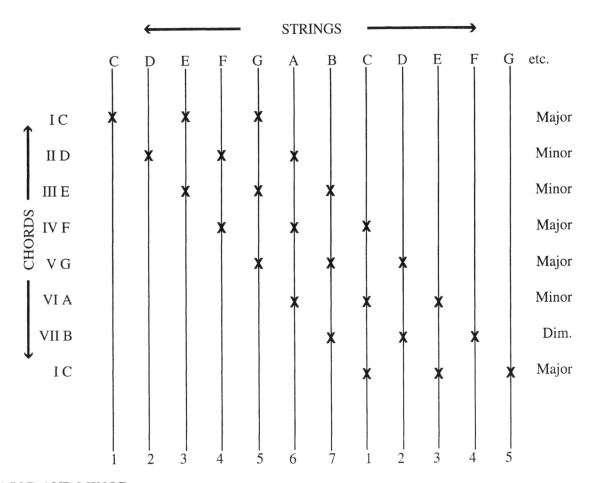

MAJOR AND MINOR

You will notice a different characteristic sound to some of the chords. Look at the right of the chart. You will see that the C, or I chord is called "major." The D, or II, chord is called "minor," and so on.

The major chords in our diatonic scale are I, IV, and V. The minor chords are II, III, and VI. In a C scale, they are as follows:

C major
D minor
E minor
F major
G Major
A minor

(Note the "dim." for the VII chord (B). This means "diminished." We will not be dealing with diminished chords in this book. For more complete information beyond the beginning level, please consult any book on music theory.)

You can play in a major key AND in a minor key without retuning your harp. You have three major chords and three minor chords to work with. Some tunes will utilize all minor chords, some all major, and yet others will have some of both.

In the next section, you will be playing a tune that is in a minor key yet utilizes both minor and major chords.

KEYS

How do you know what key a tune is in? The easiest way to figure this out is to find out what note ends the tune. Most often, that ending note will be the TONIC, a sort of "anchor" note which defines the key. If a tune ends with an A note, and you are tuned to a C scale, a quick look at the chart will reveal that A is minor. Therefore you are in the key of A Minor.

The following tune is in A Minor.

Section 17: Fifth Tune, "Brian Boru's March," version 1

Please notice that the tablature indicates a lilted rhythm whereas the notation does not. (This is in consideration of those who are new to reading notation.) The rhythm in the tablature is the most traditional way of playing this tune. Use this page of tablature to clarify and enhance your note-reading. Notice that there is an addition to this tablature: brackets. Please refer to section 5 for instructions on using them. Also notice that the first measure has only one beat. This should be counted as the sixth beat so the first two measures would be counted: "six, one, two, three, four, five, six".

Whether you are reading tablature or notation at this point, you have probably gained enough familiarity with it so that a step-by-step description is no longer necessary. General instructions for this tune are:

PART A: The tune consists of a repeating pattern of melody notes leading to a final phrase which "resolves" the melody. The left hand plays chords.

PART B: Three phrases which sound alike but contain important differences lead to a final phrase which mimics that of part A. The left hand plays chords.

43

Section 18: Rolled, Broken and Open Chords

A "rolled" chord is one in which the notes are played in quick succession. This is the technique that creates the characteristic sound for which harps are best known. To roll a chord, place the fingers on the strings and pull off quickly and smoothly from lowest to highest note.

Some harpers find they must move each finger separately, in the usual plucking motion; others do well by using wrist motion and keeping the fingers stable. Whichever way works for you, you can count on its requiring practice and patience. Strive for a smooth rolled sound in which all the notes of the chord can be heard separately but not individually.

The sound of a rolled chord is more interesting than that of a chord in which all the notes are plucked simultaneously. When playing the harp you will switch from one effect to the other for variety.

The symbol for a rolled chord is a squiggly line beside the chord notation (see the music and tablature examples below).

A "broken" chord is one in which the notes are played separately to create a rhythm. The rhythm created by breaking a chord in various ways depends upon the time signature of the piece. Below are some examples to show how breaking a chord into its component notes can create different types of rhythms.

As we have seen, the most basic form of a chord is 1-3-5. The example given of that form was a C chord, or I chord. This form is called a TRIAD. All chords are triads when played in their **most basic** form. However, it is possible to play chords in more interesting ways.

For instance, you could eliminate the middle note, simply playing an interval of a fifth. Or you could play 1-3-5-8, using fingers #4, 3, 2, and 1. We call that a "full" chord.

Or you could play 1-5-8 without the 3. This is called an "open" chord. Try this exercise:

With the left hand, place fingers 4, 3, 2, and 1 on CEGC, and pluck them all at the same time. Now place them again and roll them. Now place them once more and pluck them one at a time. (This is a full chord.) Now switch hands and repeat.

Now place fingers 4, 2, and 1 on CGC. (This is an open chord.) Play it all three ways as you did the full chord, then switch hands and repeat.

Some types of music use open chords rather than full ones. In Section 19 you will find a variation on "Brian Boru's March" and it uses rolled, broken, and open chords.

Rolled Chords (Etude to the tune of "Greensleeves")

Broken Chords (Etude to the tune of "Simple Gifts")

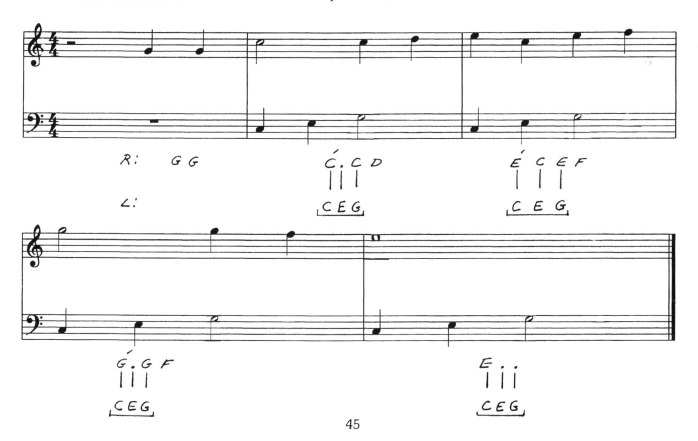

Interval, Full Chord, and Open Chord
Example Chart

String No.	String Name	(Triad) Basic C Chord	Third	Fifth	Full Chord	Open Chord	Open Chord
8	C				●	●	●
7	B						
6	A						
5	G	●		●	●	●	
4	F						
3	E	●	●		●		●
2	D						
1	C	●	●	●	●	●	●

The Triad, Full Chord, and Open Chords are all forms of a C Chord. This same principle is true of any chord.

Section 19: Variation on "Brian Boru's March" version 2

This version uses broken and rolled chords.

Trad. Irish

Section 20: Sixth Tune, "Nonesuch"

This is a tune from Medieval times. The left hand plays intervals rather than chords (two notes at a time instead of three or more). The specific interval used is a fifth. As you can see, fifths can be played in many positions. As long as there is a distance of five notes, it is a fifth no matter where it starts.

You will notice that the interval of a fifth has an ancient sound. This is the kind of harmony that was preferred in Medieval times and earlier.

Trad. English

48

Section 21: Levers

If your harp has levers, surely you have wondered what they are for. These are the devices installed at the top of some or all of the strings, which flip or turn up and down to change the pitch of the string. When they are flipped up, they provide "sharps" by raising the pitch of the string 1/2 step. Thus you can retune your harp quickly into different keys or achieve "accidentals," which are sharped notes within a tune. (NOTE: "sharped" is the correct term, not "sharpened.")

When all your levers are down, your harp is tuned to a C scale, if you followed the tuning instructions at the beginning of this book. But when you flip levers, you change that scale.

For instance, if you flip your F levers, the diatonic scale now begins on G. G becomes 1.

G	A	B	C	D	E	F♯	G
1	2	3	4	5	6	7	8(1)

TRANSPOSING

Any tune that you played using the C scale can be played using the G scale if you simply think of the string NUMBERS. If you played a tune using chords I, IV, and V, those chords remain in the same position in the new scale and are still I, IV, and V. In the key of C the I, IV, and V chords were C, F, and G. In the key of G the I, IV, and V chords are G, C, and D. See the tune below for an example. Moving a tune from one key to another is called TRANSPOSING. In the example tune we transpose from the key of C to the key of G.

First play the tune in C with all the levers down. Then flip up your F levers for the transposed version. Notice the ♯ on the staff.

Sally Gardens

Trad. Irish

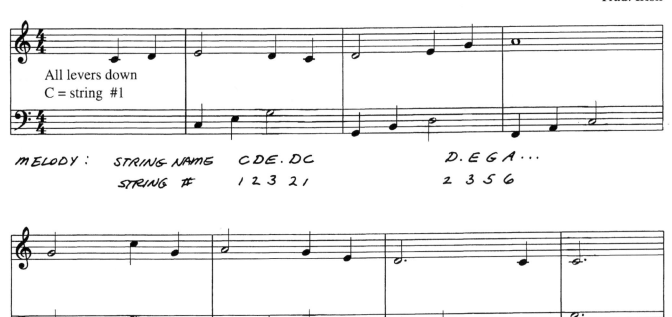

50

Now we will transpose the same tune into the key of G, and then the key of D. Simply flip your F levers up for the key of G. Then also flip your C levers up for the key of D.

Sally Gardens Example – Transposed to G

F lever sharped
G = string #1

Right Hand   *G A B .*   *A G A .*   *B D E . . .*
Finger No.s   *1 2 3*   *2 1 2*   *3 5 6*

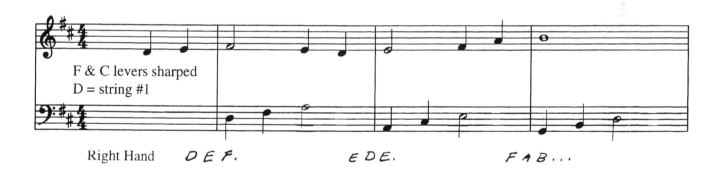

D . G D E .   *D B A . .*   *G G . . .*
5 8 5 6   *5 3 2*   *1 1*

Sally Gardens Example – Transposed to Key of D

F & C levers sharped
D = string #1

Right Hand   *D E F .*   *E D E .*   *F A B . . .*

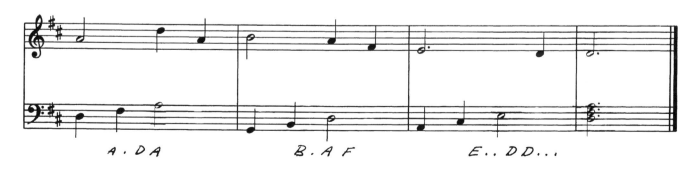

A . D A   *B . A F*   *E . . D D . . .*

51

Lever Chart

Vertical lines are the strings.
Dark grey areas indicate flipped levers.
When a lever is flipped, the note becomes sharped.

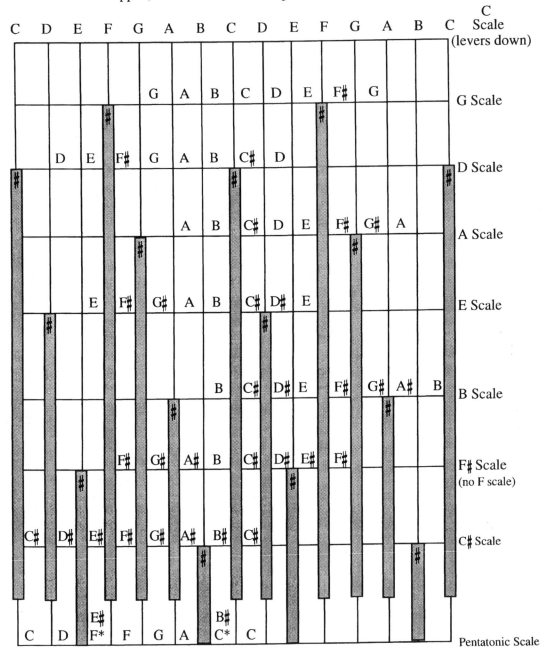

*E♯ is the same as F.
 B♯ is the same as C.

Section 22: Octave Jumps

Sometimes harpers complain that it is difficult to accurately play a chord and then move up to another chord that is not close to the first one. Actually it is not difficult at all; they just don't know a simple secret. Look at the exercise below. You will see that your left hand plays a note or chord and then jumps two full octaves and plays the same chord again, but higher. Remember, rests in the notation simply mean don't play those beats.

Place the left-hand and right-hand fingers. DON'T PLAY IT YET. Now look at the strings on which you will play the third note or chord. You now have your fingers in one place and your eyes in another. KEEP YOUR EYES ON THE THIRD NOTE OR CHORD, and pluck the first. (Did you forget and look at your fingers as they plucked? Try again. It is not necessary to watch your fingers pluck; if you have pre-placed them you cannot make a mistake!) Keeping your eyes on the third note or chord, pluck the second. Then place the *fourth* and play the *third* while looking at the *fifth*. And so on. Your eyes are never on the chord you are plucking. They are always ahead.

Leapfrog

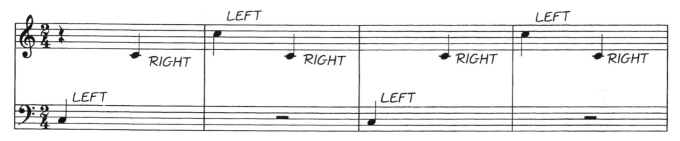

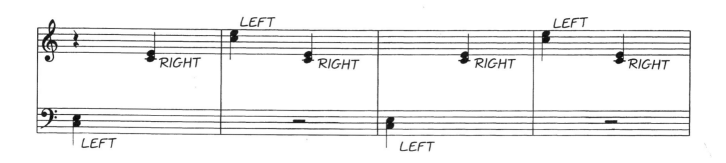

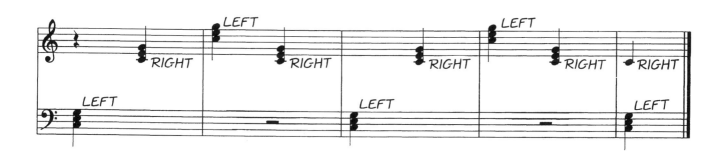

Section 23: Ninth Tune, "Return from Fingall"

There are two eighth notes per beat.

R: É D C B Á B C D   É D C B Á ...   D́ C B D Ǵ . D .   É . D . Ǵ ...
     | | | | |
     E   E   D   E   D
L: A   A   G   A   G

R: É D C B Á B C D   É D C B Á ...   D́ C B D Ǵ . B C   B́ . A . Á ...
     | | | | |
     E   E   D   D   E
L: A   A   G   G   A

Section 24: Ornaments

An ornament is a note or notes, usually played with the right hand, in addition to the melody, for the purpose of enhancing melody or accenting certain parts of it. Some ornaments are simple; others more complicated.

Unfortunately, there is no set terminology applying to ornaments; each teacher has his or her own descriptive word for each one.

We will look at two simple ornaments here. We will call them "runs" and "grace notes."

A "run" in this book is a group of rapidly ascending or descending notes ending on a melody note.

A "grace note" is a note occurring just before a melody note and played so quickly that it cannot be construed as part of the melody, and it does not take any extra beats. An ornament is never counted in the beats.

To execute the run in the example below, place fingers 4, 3, 2, and 1 on the consecutive strings shown, and pluck from lowest note to highest in quick succession, emphasizing the last note. (This is the same type of motion we used for rolled chords, except this group of notes is not a chord in this case.)

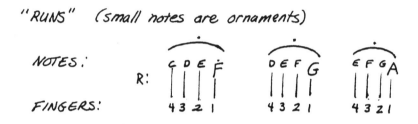

To execute the grace notes in the examples below, place fingers 1 and 2 on the notes indicated and play them in quick succession, emphasizing the second note.

"GRACE NOTES"

R: ᴮC ᴬC ᴬD ᴮD
    1 2 1 2 1 2 1 2

Section 25: "The Grace Note Waltz"

Grace Note Waltz

Remember: ornaments do not take up any extra beats.

More Tunes to Learn

Mist – Covered Mountains

Finger numbers and brackets appear above or below the notes.

means cross over with thumb to next note

Trad. Celtic

Part A

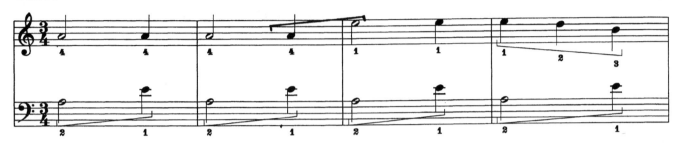

Continue to place left hand
Intervals with fingers 2 - 1.

Part B

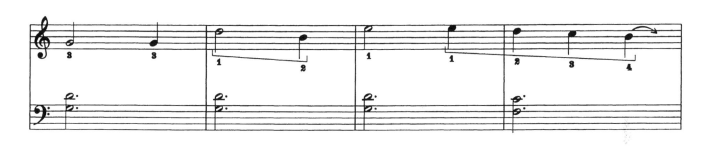

Tha Mi Sgith (I Am So Tired)

Trad. Irish

Part A

Continue to place left-hand intervals with
fingers 2–1.

60

Part B

Castle Kelly

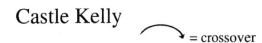

= crossover

Trad. Irish

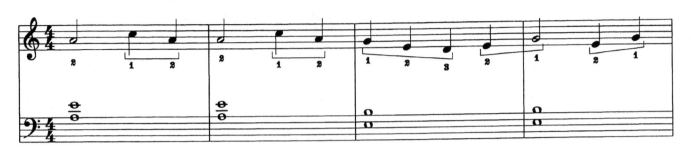

same fingerings

(throughout)

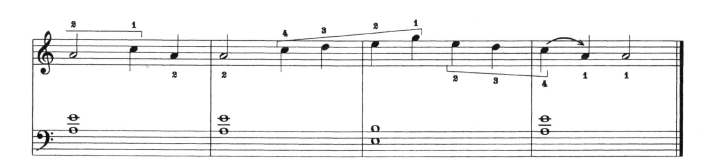

63

The Rushes

Trad. Scottish

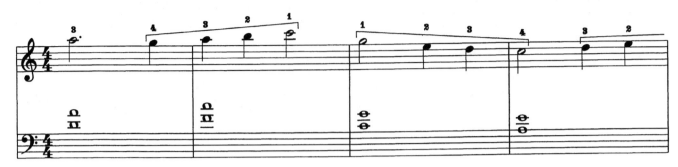

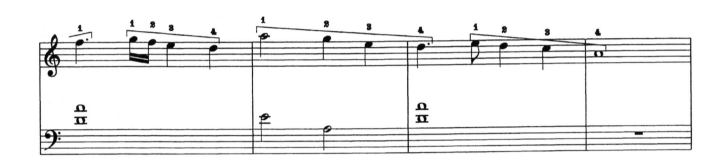

same fingering

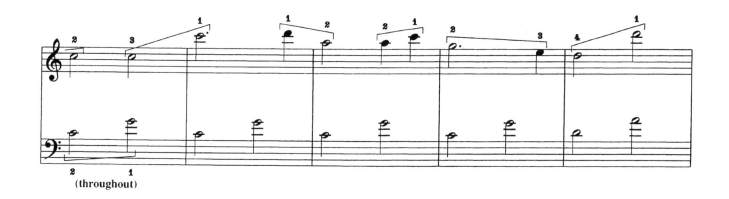

(throughout)

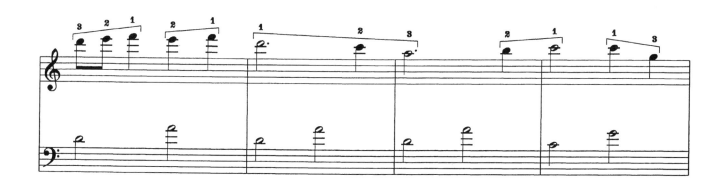

Sally Gardens

Part A

Trad. Irish

same fingerings – (Part A Repeat)

Part B

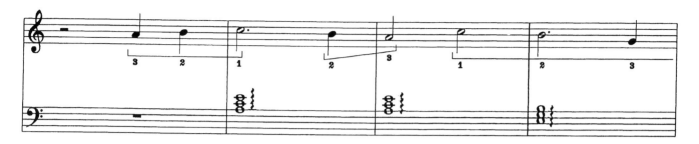

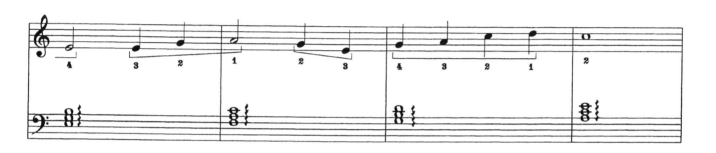

same fingerings as Part A

Campbell's Farewell

Part A   Remember: grace notes do not take extra beats.   Trad. Scottish

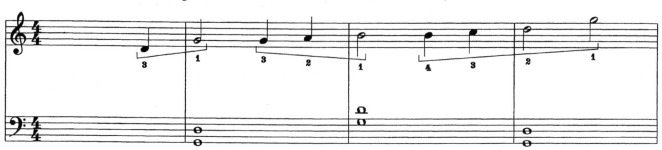

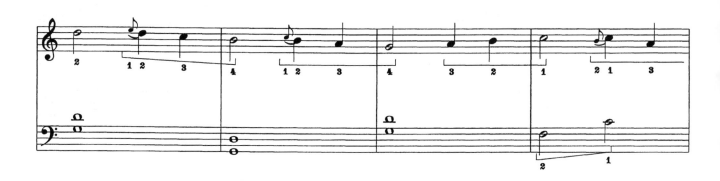

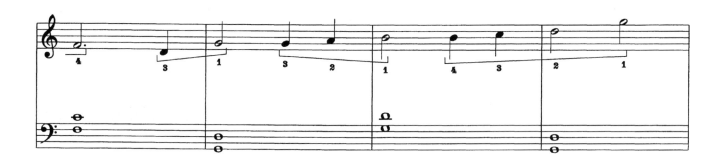

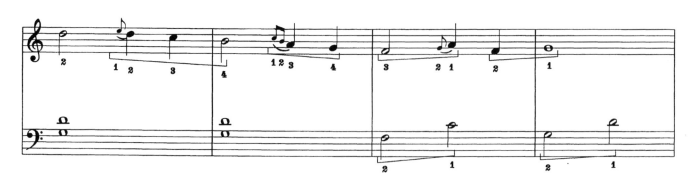

Part B

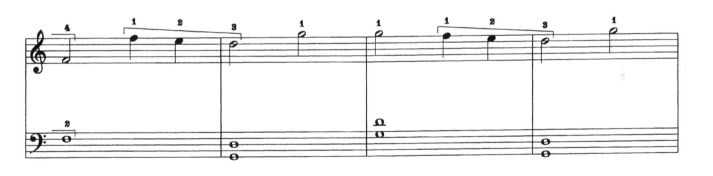

Flowers Of Edinburgh

(Key of G: Flip up your F levers)

Trad. Scottish

with fingering brackets

Part B

71

Parson's Farewell

Trad. Scottish

Lovely Joan

Trad. English

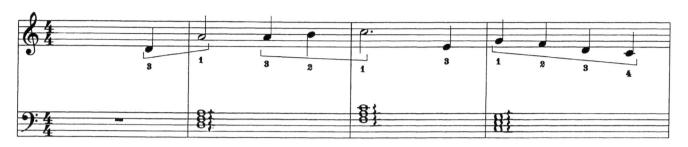

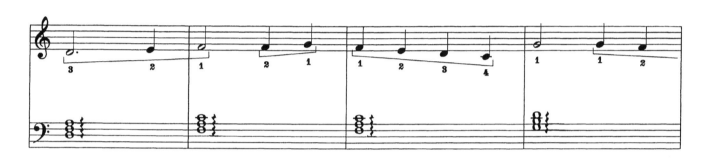

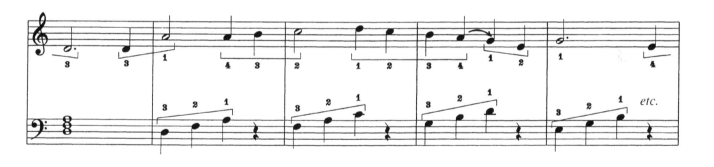

etc.

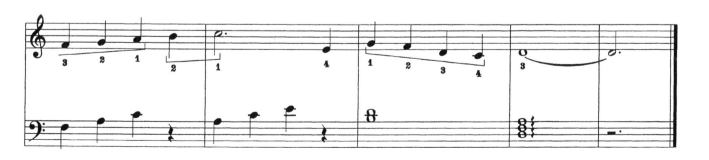

Round The Horn

Trad. English

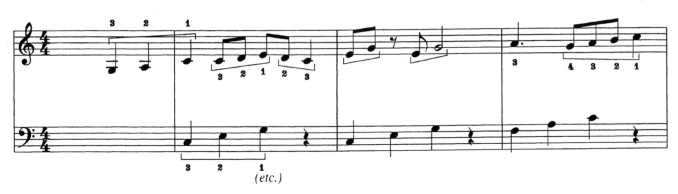

(etc.)

Glossary

bracket   Symbols showing how many and which fingers to place in advance of playing a passage of music.

broken chord   A chord which is played by plucking the notes separately (rather than all at once or by rolling); often for the purpose of creating a rhythm.

crossover   A movement in which the thumb crosses over a placed finger and is placed on a lower string before the finger plucks.

crossunder   A movement in which a finger crosses under the placed thumb and is placed on a higher string before the thumb plucks.

etude   A short piece of music played for the purpose of developing specific skills related to movement and control of the hands and fingers.

full chord   A chord using the intervals of 1-3-5-8.

grace note   An ornamental note occurring just before a melody note and played so quickly that it cannot be construed as part of the melody.

hand position   The way in which the hands are held while playing the harp.

harp   Any of a family of stringed instruments having a soundbox, pillar, and neck from which several or many strings are stretched across a distance to meet the soundbox at a right angle, and which is played by plucking the strings with the fingertips or fingernails.

hornpipe   A lively, lilting dance originating in Ireland.

lever   A device installed near the top of a harp string, which, when engaged, sharps the string 1/2 step.

march   A brisk musical piece in 2/4, 4/4 or 6/8 time, originally used to create a beat to which soldiers could walk in unison.

notation   A musical score from which the notes, time signature and rhythm are read.

octave   An interval of an eighth, i.e. from C to C or from G to G.

open chord   A chord played in a form other than the basic intervals of 1-3-5 or 1-3-5-8; i.e. 1-5-8 or 1-3-8 or 1-5-10.

ornament   A note or group of notes played in addition to a melody for the purpose of enhancing it or emphasizing some part or aspect of it.

placement   The positioning of fingers on the strings prior to plucking.

plucking   The act of making a string resonate by squeezing the string and then pulling the finger off it.

rolled chord   A chord which is played by plucking in quick succession the notes from lowest to highest, or sometimes from highest to lowest, rather than all at once.

run   In this book, the term "run" refers to an ornament which consists of a group of rapidly ascending or descending notes ending on a melody note.

tablature	An alternative method of reading notation for music.
tone	The quality of the sound of a plucked string or the sound of an instrument.
transposing	The act of playing or writing a tune in a key other than its original one.
tuning	Adjusting the pitch of the strings of the harp (or other instrument).
variation	A version of a musical piece or passage which resembles the original but differs in some way.
waltz	A musical piece in 3/4 time; a dance set to that music.

About the Author

Laurie Riley has been performing, adjudicating, and teaching harp internationally for over twenty years. Her numerous recordings, books, and videos are standards in the lever harp world. She plays and teaches several types of harps; this book serves as basic instruction for all styles.

Laurie has been featured on NPR's All Things Considered, as well as in concert accompanying The Chieftains. Her music has been featured on American Airlines and on the well-known Narada Collections. Her recordings can be heard on radio stations worldwide.

Other books available from Mel Bay authored by Laurie Riley include "Wedding Music for the Lever Harp", "You Can Teach Yourself to Play Lever Harp", and "Celtic Music for the Folk Harp".

Please visit Laurie's website at www.laurieriley.com

Laurie can also be reached at PO Box 1563, Sedona AZ 86339

Great Music at Your Fingertips

47167389R00046

Made in the USA
Lexington, KY
29 November 2015